GERMANY

Europe

Gospel and Culture pamphlets:

1. S. Wesley Ariarajah, *An Ongoing Discussion in the Ecumenical Movement*

2. Stan McKay and Janet Silman, *The First Nations of Canada*

3. Ion Bria, *Romania*

4. Noel Davies, *Wales*

5. James Massey, *Panjab*

6. Antonie Wessels, *Secularized Europe*

7. Israel Selvanayagam, *Tamilnadu*

8. Ambrose Moyo, *Zimbabwe*

9. John Pobee, *West Africa*

10. Lewin L. Williams, *The Caribbean*

11. Donald E. Meek, *The Scottish Highlands*

12. Allan K. Davidson, *Aotearoa New Zealand*

13. *Germany*

14. *Women's Perspectives*

15. K.M. George, *The Early Church*

GOSPEL AND CULTURES PAMPHLET 13

GERMANY

*Seeking a Relevant Witness
Beyond Contrast and Assimilation*

**An ecumenical
study group**

WCC Publications, Geneva

This pamphlet is an adapted English version of a German original published by the Evangelisches Missionswerk in Deutschland (EMW), under the title *Schritt halten mit Gott: Das Evangelium und unsere Kultur*, EMW-informationen No. 110/1996, Breklum, 1995. The members of the EMW study group on "The Gospel and Our Culture" which prepared the text were Theodor Ahrens, Sebastian Borck, Theo Christiansen, Hartwig Helfritz, Carlos Hoch, Volker Küster, Ingo Lembke, Ulrich Luig, Herbert Meissner, Bettina Opitz-Chen, Friederike Raum-Blöcher, Klaus Roeber, Rüdiger Sachau, Klaus Schäfer, Wolfram Suhr, Rainer Wassner and Joachim Wietzke. Editor: Brunhild Christmann; English translation by Alexander Page.

Cover design: Edwin Hassink
Cover illustration: A recent Kirchentag (epd-bild/Mehrl)

ISBN 2-8254-1207-4

© 1996 WCC Publications, 150 route de Ferney,
1211 Geneva 2, Switzerland

No. 13 in the Gospel and Cultures series

Printed in Switzerland

Table of Contents

vii INTRODUCTION

1 1. THE MYTH OF THE "CHRISTIAN OCCIDENT"

10 2. AFTER 1945: THE "ESTABLISHED VOLKS-KIRCHE" AND THE "CHURCH IN SOCIALISM"

20 3. WHERE WE STAND TODAY

30 4. NEW TESTAMENT PERSPECTIVES

36 5. THE CHURCH'S RESPONSE: TWO MODELS

46 6. INCULTURATION OF THE GOSPEL IN CONCILIAR PERSPECTIVE

Introduction

For many centuries the Western European Roman Catholic and Protestant traditions of Christianity were considered an adequate expression of the relation between the gospel and cultures. This was even the case in many cultures outside Western Europe whose encounter with the gospel occurred as a result of the missionary expansion of the church. Despite a general awareness that Christianity had evolved from a long process of inculturation with roots in the Judaic, Graeco-Hellenistic and Roman cultures since the Middle Ages and even into this century, the cultural synthesis of Occidental Christianity was seen as synonymous with the universal *corpus christianum*. Consequently, the expansion of Christianity to other cultural spheres was reduced to a problem of simply modifying the proclamation of the gospel — which was in fact the gospel in Western garments — to other cultures.

This Eurocentric viewpoint was shaken to the core by the first world war and collapsed entirely in the wake of the second world war. During the subsequent process of decolonization, Christians of the Southern hemisphere not only rejected the claim of those in the West to represent the universal expression of the gospel, but also rediscovered their own cultural traditions. This opened up the possibility of developing an original and independent theology and a definition of the church which went far beyond the mere adaptation of Western Christianity to other cultural traditions.

While this was going on, churches in the West were arriving at a deeper understanding of how their theology and ecclesiastical practice were conditioned and shaped by their own cultural heritage. Already the Enlightenment, with its increasing awareness of the "other" and "alien", had challenged naive earlier assumptions and led to a recognition of the relativity of European culture. But only now was it possible to recognize and accept more fully that all cultures are equal in rank over against the gospel and that the gospel must find adequate expression through each individual culture.

At the outset this new discussion on the relationship between gospel and cultures was primarily concerned with the methodological problem of identifying points of contact with other cultures in order to communicate the gospel more effectively within non-Western cultures. More recently, the main weight of the argument has shifted to the theological issue of how to find the appropriate form and expression of gospel as "good news" in different cultural settings, given the fact that the gospel always encounters these new settings in a specific cultural expression from outside.

One aspect of the discussion of gospel and cultures or gospel and society is that it in no way implies an uncritical acceptance of or identification with one's own culture or the prevalent culture, but focuses instead upon transforming the prevailing culture through the spirit of the gospel.

Since the 1970s this dialectical relationship between gospel and culture — on the one hand the rediscovery of indigenous culture, on the other the critical position vis-à-vis all forms of culture — has dominated the discussion at the assemblies and major mission conferences of the World Council of Churches. At the 1975 assembly in Nairobi, for example, it was stated that Jesus Christ "affirms and shapes every culture". A document prepared for the 1980 world mission conference in Melbourne posed the question: "What help can we gain from the gospel in developing a constructive yet critical orientation towards our culture?" While the ecumenical discussion of the relationship between gospel and culture has constantly followed this line of argument, it was clear from the WCC's seventh assembly (Canberra 1991) and in the controversy that ensued — not least over the presentation by Professor Chung Hyun-Kyung — that satisfactory answers to the dilemma have yet to be found.

This has encouraged our working group to take part in the regional and national study process on gospel and cultures, commissioned by the WCC in preparation for the 1996 international missionary conference in Salvador de Bahia, Brazil, under the theme "Called to One Hope — the Gospel in Diverse Cultures". In view of the ecumenical discussion, we feel that as Christians in Germany we have a responsibility to share with the ecumenical family some of our current thinking and historical experience in relation to the interaction of gospel and cultures. It has been our concern to reflect on the different experiences of the church in East and West Germany; and we believe that the transformation of the social situation following German reunification calls for a reappraisal of society and culture. We have sought to encourage a debate about the position of the church within our culture and the inculturation of the gospel within our own sphere of life.

In our discussions we have focused on the following key themes:

— *Our own ecclesiastical-cultural heritage*: What is the history of the encounter between gospel and culture which we come from as Protestant Christians in Germany?[1]
— *Processes of cultural change in our own sphere of life*: What challenges do we face with respect to our witness to the gospel in our culture?
— *The direction of genuine and responsible proclamation of the gospel in our situation*: Which criteria need to be observed in all our efforts within the inculturation process?
— *The position of the church towards cultural challenges raised within our own context*: Which trends and aspects of a missionary presence of the church in our society are under discussion today and what significance can be attached to them?

Other important questions — such as the cultural captivity of European and German theology, which only became apparent with the emergence of contextual theology in the Third World, or the issue of how to achieve ecumenical consensus given the very different cultural expressions of the gospel — have been accorded subordinate status in this study.[2] The present pamphlet represents only part of an ongoing discussion. We hope it will stimulate further thinking on these critical topics.

NOTES

[1] While our discussion is limited to Protestantism, Catholic perspectives can be found in G. Evers, "Inculturation as New Evangelization: A Challenge to European Theology", and L. Bertsch SJ, "Inculturation in Europe's Societal Situation: An Introduction", both in *Jahrbuch für Kontextuelle Theologien*, no. 94, Frankfurt, IKO-Verlag für Interkulturelle Kommunikation, 1994, pp.73-100; 101-11; and in K. Gabriel, "Christentum zwischen Tradition und Postmoderne", *Questiones Disputatae*, no.141, Freiburg/Basel/Vienna, 1992.

[2] Cf. Th. Ahrens, "Christentum im Dialog der Kulturen: Eine westeuropäische Perspektive", *Zeitschrift für Missionswissenschaft und Religionswissenschaft*, Vol. 79, no. 1, 1995, pp.27-42.

1. The Myth of the "Christian Occident"

From its early beginnings Christianity was a religion characterized by missionary outreach. After the resurrection Jesus commanded the disciples to bear the gospel — which had its origins with Jesus in the context of Judaic culture — to all parts of the globe. Fulfilling this task meant more than simply carrying the message of salvation through Christ to other peoples and cultures. In the course of missionary outreach, the concept of the gospel was itself affected by the influence of Hellenic and Latin thought forms as well as by Germanic culture. Mission necessarily involves contact with culture, and the acceptance of the gospel always implied a concept of the gospel adapted to cultural conditions.

Over several centuries the gospel underwent a process of inculturation in Europe — centred initially on the Mediterranean region, then north of the Alps. This process led to a form of Christian culture which was later described with some pride as "the Christian Occident" or "Western Christian civilization". It was maintained that basis of this Western European culture was the synthesis of Graeco-Roman antiquity, Germanic and Christian traditions. The Roman Catholic faith and the concept of the Empire fulfilled a unifying and consolidating function. The dual pillars supporting this common culture among the peoples of Europe — this unifying *corpus christianum* — were the pope and the emperor.

Later generations maintained the image of a Christian Europe, resorting nostalgically to the concept of this earlier Western Christian civilization whenever society was confronted with periods of marked cultural change and in the face of increasing secularization. The adherents of the Romantic movement wrote passionately about the ideal of the common culture of Christian mediaeval Europe. Novalis began his essay on "Die Christenheit oder Europa" (1799) with the words: "These were wonderful, extraordinary times, when Europe was a Christian country, when Christianity was at home in this part of the globe shaped by man; a huge fellowship united even the most far-flung province in this vast and broad spiritual empire."

In reality the image of this Christian civilization owes a great deal to an idealization that bears little resemblance to historical fact. The schism that opened up between the Western and Eastern churches in 1054 testifies to a deep-seated split in European Christianity. Unity in Christian Europe had to a large extent been achieved through the powers of coercion and violence which the state invested in the church. Constantine's rule brought an end to the diversity of Christian theology. The Roman Catholic faith became the obligatory state religion with which all citizens of the empire must comply. Deviant opinion — whether within the church or among non-Christian minorities — was suppressed and crushed, even though church unity was increasingly undermined by subterranean heretical tendencies since the late Middle Ages. The antagonism between the emperor and the papacy, the political role played by the papacy during the Middle Ages and the paganism of the papacy in the Renaissance reveal the problematic character of this idealized unified Christian empire. The demise of the *corpus christianum*, if indeed it ever existed in such a form, had undoubtedly come some time before the Reformation. But it persisted as an ideal in the minds of many, exerting an influence, conscious or subconscious, as an objective for determining the proper interaction between the gospel and culture which to some extent survives even to this day.

The Reformation and the religious wars which followed in its wake resulted in a confessional and political division of this so-called Western Christian Europe and further weakened the concept of a unified *corpus christianum*. The starting point of the Reformation can be seen in the pious movements of the Middle Ages which were critical of the official Roman Catholic model of inculturation. Luther, by criticizing the way the church turned penitence into a business, challenged the claim that the church could legitimate sinners before God. The desire for a "merciful" God — in

Luther's words, the justification of the sinner — led him to an understanding of human beings as responsible subjects before God. The revolutionary concept of human conscience, something not subject to a worldly authority, and the concept of individual personality before God furnished the basis for a new awareness of freedom and responsiblity. Luther's definition of vocation, emphasizing Christian service in the world, contributed to a new ethos which taught people to shape the world.

Another extremely significant new development followed, which can be associated with the word "Enlightenment", which Kant interpreted as the "departure of man from his self-imposed subservience". Attention now centred on such values as subjectivity, individuality, autonomy and emancipation of the individual. Emphasis was now placed on the role of human creativity in shaping the destiny of the world, the idea of human progress and the advance of secularization. These ideas were the source of a fundamentally new cultural stream, which has continued to characterize Europe since then. The values of liberty, equality and fraternity proclaimed by the French Revolution of 1789 and the concepts of human rights and tolerance which it ushered in were revolutionary, representing what can be rightly called modern European culture.

The criticism of the church and the sometimes radical rejection of the Christian tradition and heritage which emerged from the Enlightenment represented an affront to the authority and self-perceived status of the church. Whereas the Middle Ages and Reformation both retained the European Christian hypothesis of the objective, indisputable existence and dutiful acceptance of God, the advent of the new age and modernity damaged the idea of the self-evidence of God. In place of a religious belief in eternal salvation through God emerged an increasing desire for temporal self-realization. The quest is now for a solution to the dilemma of human existence here and now — a way to develop humanity without the "working hypothesis of God" or at least to integrate the "working hypothesis of God" into a this-worldly understanding of salvation. This process did not simply grow out of any bad intentions; in the light of social developments the outcome was inevitable.

Even to this day, the themes of theological debate — either open or subliminal — turn around the logic of the Enlightenment, which has shaped European culture so deeply. Meanwhile, the church has long included development and progress on its banner, recognizing the significance of human rights and the values of liberty, participation, equality and solidarity, while calling for the individual to behave reasonably and take responsibility for one's own deeds and behaviour. This understanding, which touched off a lengthy process of rethinking, is now firmly anchored in our sense of mission. [1]

Not until the 19th century did the epoch of change ushered in by the Enlightenment really begin to affect a large cross-section of society. Over the course of this period a clear differentiation of thought arose along class-specific lines. For the liberal bourgeoisie the emancipatory character of the Enlightenment primarily comprised individual self-determination and fulfilment either in economic-political terms (capitalism), social-political terms (democratic or national self-determination), "ethics" (the recognition of humanization, humanity, autonomy, liberty, the concept of "self") or national determination. [2] Marxism also emphasized self-determination, but saw the cause of all the suffering of the working class in the intrinsic injustice of the economic and social structures. Thus, the workers placed their hopes in changing these. Such change must be consciously enacted by one's own strength and pursued with the aim of achieving a society in which class rule was abolished, a "classless society".

Within the Protestant church of the 19th century, the process of change outlined above was one of the factors provoking an extensive discussion of the meaning of the gospel in relation to culture — or, in the terms used at that time, the relationship of church or religion to culture. The core of this debate was the diversity of views within Protestantism on whether the Enlightenment was legitimate from a Christian standpoint. An enlightened, liberal and so-called "free" Protestantism came face to face with an anti-Enlightenment, anti-revolutionary, anti-democratic and ecclesiastical-confessional strand. The Protestant theology and religiosity anchored in the liberal bourgeoisie and liberal bourgeois values sought to mediate between the traditions of the Reformation and modern culture with its roots in the Enlightenment. This type of inculturation is recorded in theological history as "cultural Protestantism" (*Kultur-Protestantismus*).[3] Importance was now attached to the concept of nation and the vision of a new and unifying Christian-national culture, the demand for a wide-ranging reform of the church in order to make it more democratic and the jettisoning of antiquated dogmatical ballast carried over from the past. Richard Rothe formulated this process as the new "conciliation between religion and culture". Recognition was also given to the economic interests of the bourgeoisie. Ownership of the means of production received theological approval and the accumulation of capital was supported. According to Max Weber's well-known if controversial theory, it was the Calvinist form of Protestantism which produced the necessary impetus for capitalism to develop and succeed. The church came to regard itself as the expression of the bourgeoisie and its national, social, economic and ethical norms, such as conscience, commitment to duty and humanitarianism. Conservative circles within the church, as well as the church establishment, despised this attempt at inculturation, dismissing the form of Christianity that resulted in such terms as "liberal compromised Christianity", "humanistic Protestantism", "reductionist Protestantism" or simply as a "cultural faith", "cultural religion" or "cultural Christianity".

While this cultural Protestantism was firmly rooted in the social and moral milieu of the bourgeoisie and the institutional confessional Protestantism maintained a staunchly anti-enlightened, anti-revolutionary standpoint, the church was becoming increasingly detached from the proletariat, which was under the influence of social-democratic and Marxist thinking. The workers represented those layers of society which had no share in the prosperity of the bourgeoisie or indeed any material security. Apart from the initiative of the "Inner Mission" (*Innere Mission*) in the area of social service and mission in the community, the church showed little interest in or sympathy for the emancipatory movements of the working class and willingly accepted a synthesis of bourgeoisie, nation and capital. Consequently, it was no surprise that the working class felt alienated from the church and adopted an anti-clerical tenor. There simply was no inculturation of the gospel in the culture of the working class or in relation to its existential situation. And the attempt years later to inculturate the gospel in the world of the industrial working class in the form of "religious socialism" received only minority support and therefore could not succeed.

The demise of the monarchy after the first world war threw German Protestantism into disarray. The old alliance of throne and altar had been brought to an abrupt end, and the privileges of the church were curtailed. The mainstream of German Protestantism found it difficult to come to terms with this. The security of former times was sorely missed. Democracy and the liberal and socialist ideas of the Weimar Republic were met with distrust. The monarchy was nostalgically recalled. Thus the development of a political theology based on the concept of nation and the national church came as no surprise. Basically conservative, nationalist, anti-democratic and increasingly anti-Semitic, its motives were — at least in some sectors of Protestantism — evangelistic and religious. The theological guideline was the concept of nation or *Volk*, of a specifically German national character or national spirit, which was often perceived as a natural or God-given quality and order of things. It was hoped that this concept of inculturation — the church rooted in the nation or *Volk*, or, as it was occasionally described, the modernization of Christianity through Germanization — would bring both the working class and intelligentsia back into the fold of church and community, thus combating the individualism which was regarded as having a corrupting influence.

Seen from this perspective, it is perhaps not surprising that at least initially large sections of German Protestantism welcomed the emergence of the National Socialist movement and its taking of power in 1933. National Socialism appeared to give religion new impetus, because Hitler's party seemed to support positive Christianity. Party members attended worship services wearing their uniforms and bearing their banners. They married ostentatiously in the church. Many people saw this national people's movement, with its religious undertones, as a means of bringing the gospel to the German masses. Seeing a mass movement embracing all layers of society, the church did not want once again to miss an opportunity to inculturate the gospel.

Following this logic, the *Glaubensbewegung Deutsche Christen* ("Faith Movement of German Christians"), established in 1932, drew up a programme highly similar to that of Hitler's party: "We commit ourselves to a positive, natural Christian faith in keeping with the German Lutheran spirit and heroic piety."

To be sure, it did not take long for many in the ministry and among the laity to recognize that the synthesis of the gospel and German culture propounded by Hitler and the "German Christians" was not merely a distortion but nothing less than the betrayal of the gospel. Unequivocal criticism of this assimilation of racist ideology into evangelical theology was clearly formulated by Karl Barth, who had already opposed the tendencies of cultural Protestantism and rejected on theological grounds any synthesis of the gospel and culture. Barth based his argument on the concept of the freedom of the gospel: the gospel is the word of God, free from the influence of human beings, not seeking points of contacts with any culture. The gospel meets humankind as a stranger from without: it speaks a foreign word but makes itself understood. This theology found its clearest expression in the Barmen Theological Declaration of May 1934, drawn up by the Confessing Church against the German nationalists' distortion of the gospel. The Barmen Declaration, which took issue with any attempt to submit the gospel to the imperative of a specific national or nationalist culture or to interpret it on the basis of a nationalist explanation of history, concluded: "We reject the false teaching, as if the church could or must recognize as source of its proclamation apart or besides the one word of God still other events and powers, forms and truths as revelation of God."

The traumatic experience of the false teaching propagated by the "German Christians" would continue to determine church thinking in Germany long after the war. The assumption was that, with the rejection of the nationalist theology by the Barmen Declaration, the whole question of culture and history and the reflection of the social and political context of the gospel could be dismissed from theological debate and thinking.[4] Nowhere else in the world was such a taboo placed on the whole question of the church and its adaptation to social, economic, political conditions and other factors or trends in society as in (West) Germany. The consequences of this can be clearly traced up until recent history and following the unification of the German church after 1989.

NOTES

[1] See Th. Ahrens, *op. cit.*, p.30.
[2] K.H. Ohlig, *Fundamentalchristologie: Im Spannungsfeld von Christentum und Kultur*, Munich, Kösel, 1986, p.527.

[3] On cultural Protestantism cf. F.W. Graf, "Kulturprotestantismus", *Theologische Realenzylclopädie*, Vol. 20, Berlin, W. de Gruyter, 1990, pp.230-43. A different position, especially with reference to the theology of Karl Barth, is expounded by Christoph Gestrich, *Neuzeitliches Denken und die Spaltung der dialektischen Theologie*, Tübingen, 1977.

[4] See Ernst Lange, "Von der 'Anpassung' der Kirche", in *Kirche für die Welt*, Munich, Kaiser, 1981, pp.161-76.

2. After 1945: The "Established Volkskirche" and the "Church in Socialism"

Because of the differing development of East and West Germany after 1945 the church itself diverged despite attempts to maintain its unity.

From the outset the church in West Germany met with favourable conditions and benefited from a democratic constitution which allowed it to develop freely and participate in the political process with its own ideas, thus bringing the gospel into the public debate. In the words of U. Ruh,

> Both on the Catholic and Protestant side the hope was repeatedly expressed that there would be a widespread re-Christianization of a society that had been ideologically disoriented and shaken to its foundations by National Socialism and war. As a consequence, the Protestant church regarded itself as a church open to all layers and groups in society, which by recalling its former heritage hoped to restore moral values and encourage the ethical and moral reconstruction of society.[1]

After 1945 the period of National Socialist rule was almost universally regarded as the zenith of a general cultural crisis, "an unparalleled cultural collapse" caused by the emancipation of human reason from divine authority and the separation of culture from its Christian foundations. Catholic and Protestant theologians alike viewed National Socialism as the logical conclusion of the "secularism" observed in all European societies which destroyed the foundation of Western Christian culture. This "crisis of culture", interpreted as God's judgment, could be overcome only by the re-Christianization of all public life. In the context of the unfolding East-West conflict, both the Christian parties which formed the postwar governments and the churches — the overwhelmingly conservative Protestant Church and the Roman Catholic Church alike — saw "Christian culture" as the decisive obstacle to Bolshevism and socialism.[2] During the 1950s it was widely accepted by Protestant thinkers that the social market economy and such values as industriousness, fulfilment of duty and respect for authority were also elements of "Christian culture". Only a small minority seemed aware that here too the gospel, and with it the church, might be used to serve political interests.

In the West, the Federal Republic of Germany expressly welcomed the role of the church as the vehicle and interpreter of the Western Christian cultural heritage which was also intended as the foundation of the state structure. The exact nature of this relationship between church and state is set forth in the legal agreement concluded between the state and the church. This gave the Protestant and Roman Catholic churches, as well as some other religious communities, the legal status of public corporations within the Federal Republic, thus maintaining continuity with the Weimar Republic and the earlier constitutional clauses on the legal position of the church in German society. Few other countries practise this combination of separation and co-operation in relation to church and state, in which the latter commits itself to strict neutrality in all matters of religion and to the protection of the right to worship, while bestowing on the church privileges which afford it an important status within society. Essential to this is the system of church taxation, by which the state authorities levy a tax on church members in addition to income tax. It is important to recognize that revenue from the church tax currently accounts for between 70 and 90 percent of the income of the Protestant dioceses and parishes in the federal states of the former West Germany. Thus the church in Germany "has a financial base far superior to that of most Christian churches in other European countries. Largely due to the church tax, most churches [in the western federal states] are extremely 'affluent' and possess an impressive infrastructure."[3]

In addition, the church enjoys the right to determine the content of religious instruction, which is guaranteed in state schools. Professors of theology, who provide theological education for students entering the ministry at state universities, are state-financed. Pastoral care within the armed forces is provided by chaplains who for the entire duration of their service have the status of civil servants. Furthermore, the state and the church co-operate closely in social and charitable work as well as in providing development aid. Finally, the church is guaranteed broadcasting time for religious programmes in the publicly-owned radio and television networks.

Co-operation with the state enables the church to reach a broad public within society. There is an extensive parish system, and the sound financial situation makes it possible to carry out widespread pastoral and welfare work within the community. Moreover, the church can support churches and development projects outside Western Europe. To be sure, this co-operation has an extremely ambivalent character, because it implies that the church is somewhat tied to the state and the sectors of influence within society. The church is thus exposed to the danger of assimilation. Even though the separation of church and state provides a constitutional guarantee of freedom of expression and action, this affinity with the state, as well as the close links between the church and the middle classes, might nurture a tendency to consider certain themes and topics as taboo. With pluralism exerting an increasing influence in recent years, the church is increasingly at risk of diffusing its identity in the efforts to reflect the various social and political options that have become common currency in society.

This ambivalence also characterized the specifically West German expressions of diaconal service. Together with other welfare organizations in West Germany the Christian welfare organizations have unquestionably made a major and worthy contribution towards defining the form of social work and welfare activities. In so doing they have occupied a broad field of activity. At the same time, fulfilling this role has involved the acceptance of public funding, participation in the state insurance system and involvement within state structures. So great is the resulting dependency on the state that it is difficult if not impossible to distinguish between the state system and the other welfare bodies. What was once provided out of a sense of duty and commitment inspired by the gospel has become a social service guaranteed as a legal right by the state. Ironically, it is through its sense of duty and service that the church has placed itself in these fetters. For this reason, the call for a more pronounced religious profile has arisen from all quarters.

A comprehensive review of Protestantism in West Germany is obviously far beyond the scope of this pamphlet. Suffice it to say that the largely restorative-conservative society in which the church found itself in the 1950s soon experienced a process of rapid transformation which inevitably left its mark on the church but in which the church was often also a driving force.[4] Various processes of modernization led to the disintegration of modern capitalist industrial society and the traditional status of work and family. The consequent change in the direction of cultural pluralism and individualism put the churches in an entirely new situation.[5] One result of this development was an erosion of the established church — with a loss of membership in the Roman Catholic Church and even more in the Protestant Church — which was especially dramatic during the 1960s. Another was a growing emphasis on religious pluralism and on a more individual form of faith. The 1960s also saw a sharp distinction emerging between two tendencies within institutional Protestantism. On the one side were those calling for comprehensive church reform, including democratization of the church, a contemporary interpretation of faith in the light of a modern scientific-technological worldview and a more decisive championing of the cause of the underprivileged of the world. On the other side were groups reflecting pietist and revivalist traditions, who saw the new movement as an attack on the integrity of the church founded on the gospel. Only in recent times has some progress been made in reconciling these two tendencies.

The debate about the future of faith and the church has continued to revolve around the very different interpretations of the meaning and reality of the *Volkskirche* — the established national, "people's" or "folk" church.[6] The latest discussions have hinged on the question which Ruh puts in these terms:

> Should the Evangelical Church in Germany remain a broad church, offering room for very different tendencies, housing different forms of piety and devotion, various expectations, degrees of loyalty and views, and regard this development as positive — or at least in today's society as inevitable — and should it base itself on the provision of a wide range of social welfare; or should it concentrate instead on bringing together determined, committed Christians and, on the basis of their piety and devoutness — or their social-political conviction and commitment — try to make a clearer statement and more decisive impact on society?[7]

What emerges from the entire discussion about the *Volkskirche* is that in German theology the controversy which once centred on the issue of gospel and culture or church and culture has now taken the form of a discussion about the meaning of the church as a church of the people — the *Volkskirche*. Or, as Graf and Tanner put it, "in the course of the permanent ecclesiological debate conducted within Federal German Protestantism, the old cultural-political controversies are pursued in a different guise".[8]

Over the last few years both the church's influence in society and the active involvement of church members has continued to decline. This erosion has had a marked effect. In the words of one observer, it is turning Christianity into a "cultural-social fringe and niche phenomenon". With the gradual disappearance of the "culture Protestantism" of the immediate post-war period, German Protestantism "generally depends on its ecclesiastical-institutional core" — with the decline of loyalty to the church in the states of the former West Germany in sharp contrast to the church's "complicated, personnel-intensive apparatus".[9] The church continues to strive within a pluralistic society to "present and convey basic values" as well as to serve as "the helping companion in crisis situations and at crucial points in human life". As a church of the people with an open commitment within pluralist society, it accepts as one of its main tasks the integration of different forms of devotion and diverse philosophies of life and political options.[10]

* * *

Whereas the church in West Germany after the second world war enjoyed privileges and high regard in public life, the situation of the church in the German Democratic Republic (GDR) was completely different. Formally, the government accepted freedom of worship, but the church was impeded in various ways and marginalized by the ideological monopoly of Marxist-Leninism. Anti-clerical and anti-religious propaganda in the 1950s was overwhelming. The state and the party attempted to discredit the church ideologically and to exert such pressure that the people would become estranged from the church. An atheistic "youth initiation ceremony" was devised as the socialist alternative to confirmation. Christians were often discriminated against in educational, training and career opportunities. The church was prevented from playing an active independent role in society or in support of social issues.

After the building of the Berlin Wall in 1961 the church adopted a different and more pragmatic approach in order to come to terms with the situation. The number of church members had been dramatically reduced. The establishment of the Federation of Evangelical Churches in the GDR and the dissolution in 1969 of structural links with the West German churches eliminated a main source of political friction with the authorities. The defensive, detached stance of the Protestant population towards the system in the GDR gave way to a process of reflection in the parishes and districts and a new orientation towards the life of Christians in the GDR. This process, which blossomed in the 1970s, is often identified by the shorthand term of "Church in Socialism". However, this does not imply that the church accommodated itself to or was in complicity with the prevailing political-ideological system. Rather, there had been "a conscious decision that the church should not oppose the socialist state but exist within it and thereby accept its implicit social responsibilities".[11] Thus, in the midst of a socialist state, the church could concern itself with evangelical freedom and self-reliance — "witness and service" in the heart of socialist society.

Within the church itself there was a variety of views concerning the "Church in Socialism". Some sectors had a generally positive attitude towards the fundamental ideas of socialism, although disagreeing with the form of socialism practised in the GDR. Others, more sceptical, viewed the formula as a necessity of life within a specific system, an unavoidable yet difficult compromise.

Although the state had revoked all of the rights of the church to act on social issues, the persistent and critical efforts of the Federation of Evangelical Churches in the GDR enabled it gradually to regain responsibilities in this area. Ecumenical relations and the human rights accords signed at the 1975 Helsinki Conference on Security and Co-operation in Europe paved the way for the church to take a stand on human rights issues and to find its place in the peace movement — both by issuing cautious synodal statements for internal church discussion and by critical public statements on justice, peace and the integrity of the creation under the umbrella of the conciliar process initiated by the World Council of Churches.

To a certain extent it was the generation of ministers who had been personally influenced by Dietrich Bonhoeffer that mapped out the difficult route — always accompanied by the threat of state repression — which led the church along the narrow path "between assimilation and insubordination".[12]

As soon as this course of action was placed on the agenda for discussion between church representatives and government officials, its inherent instability became apparent. Church pressure groups committed to such issues as peace, environmental protection and human rights were flourishing.

In the 1980s the intransigent attitude of the SED (*Sozialistische Einheitspartei Deutschlands* — the state party) towards the reforms being instituted by Mikhail Gorbachev in the Soviet Union fuelled growing frustration in the church as well as in society at large. "As the only large organization not integrated in the system, the Protestant church increasingly became a pool of critical and opposition groupings, who often used the freedom offered within the church without actually being closely involved in church life."[13]

An important turning point in the developments leading eventually to the breakdown of the GDR were the ecumenical assemblies for Justice, Peace and the Integrity of the Creation, which met three times between February 1988 and April 1989. The assemblies had a full agenda with many ideas and agreed on twelve texts which made a clear statement on the situation, including one entitled "For More Justice in the GDR".

In the immediate period leading up to the upheavals of autumn 1989, as well as during the period of transformation to a new system, the Evangelical Church played a decisive role, which was a source of amazement to many. The mighty demonstrations that took place in the cities of East Germany started with prayers for peace in the churches and represented a continuation of the traditions of the peace movement ("no violence!"). When the question of power was posed it was always the church activists who found ways to start a dialogue and who paved the way to a peaceful transformation of society. It was therefore no accident that when the Round Table met in East Berlin to discuss an interim solution, the meeting of representatives of the old political establishment and the new movement was chaired by church representatives.

* * *

Since October 1990 the Federal Republic of Germany and the German Democratic Republic have been united.

Church unity was achieved a year later. Today the euphoria with which German unification was initially greeted has given way to a more sober and thoughtful attitude and a recognition that the growing together of the two parts of Germany will take time. Social problems such as unemployment, economic reconstruction and the restoration of property to former owners in West Germany are a continuing source of frustration and bitterness.

The church of the GDR was not able to bring its experience as a minority church into the large community of the church in West Germany. The critical profile which it had adopted obviously emanated from its specific situation within a state that claimed responsibility for every area of public and social life. The affinity of the West German church with the state, its constitutionally guaranteed privileges of military chaplaincy, religious instruction in public schools and church taxation, not to mention the financial resources of its institutions all seemed alien to the churches from the GDR. The model of a church based on voluntary commitment with a critical cultural stance was developed in a minority situation. It seems to have become obsolete in a pluralist West German culture which receives the tacit support of Protestantism.

The people of the eastern federal states largely remain outside the fold of the church. There has been a huge break with tradition. It remains to be seen how the church will develop in this part of Germany — and thus in the country as a whole.

NOTES

[1] U. Ruh, *Religion und Kirche in der Bundesrepublik Deutschland*, Munich, 1990, p. 51.
[2] Cf. F.W. Graf and K. Tanner, "Kultur, Theologiegeschichtlich", in *Theologische Realenzyklopädie*, Vol. 20, pp.187-205.

³ Ruh, *op. cit*, p.81; for a more extensive treatment cf. W. Lienemann, ed., *Die Finanzen der Kirche*, Munich, Kaiser, 1989.

⁴ That the church could initiate new developments is shown by the so-called "Ostdenkschrift" of 1965: "Die Lage der Vertriebenen und das Verhältnis des deutschen Volkes zu seinen östlichen Nachbarn", in *Die Denkschriften der Evangelischen Kirche in Deutschland*, Vol. I/1, Gütersloh, EKD, 1978, pp.78-133. For the period under discussion see "Dreissig Jahre Ostdenkschrift der EKD", *epd Dokumentation*, no. 52/95, 11 Dec. 1995.

⁵ While K. Gabriel's "Christentum zwischen Tradition und Postmoderne" (*loc. cit*, esp. pp.121ff.) focuses on the Catholic Church, it is also very illuminating for the Protestant reader.

⁶ On the history of the various interpretations of this complex term see W. Huber, "Welche Volkskirche meinen wir? Ein Schlüsselbegriff gegenwärtigen Kirchenverständnisses im Licht der Barmer Theologischen Erklärung", in *Folgen christlicher Freiheit*, Neukirchen-Vluyn, 1983, pp.131-45; M. Welker "Der Mythos Volkskirche", in *Kirche und Pluralismus*, Gütersloh, 1995, pp.58-77.

⁷ U. Ruh, *op. cit*, p.60.

⁸ Graf and Tanner, *loc. cit*, p.204.

⁹ Ruh, *op. cit*, pp.61-63.

¹⁰ W. Huber, *op. cit*, pp.137ff.

¹¹ Ruh, *op. cit*, p.120.

¹² The title of the collection *Dokumente aus der Arbeit des Bundes der Evangelischen Kirchen in der DDR*, edited by Chr. Demke, M. Falkenau and H. Zeddies, Leipzig, 1994; cf. Reinhard Henkys, ed., *Die Evangelischen Kirchen in der DDR*, Munich, 1982.

¹³ Ruh, *op. cit*, p.120.

3. Where We Stand Today

Looking back at the ongoing debate on "Christianity and culture" in the 19th century, Franz Overbeck (1837-1905) concluded that "our Christianity has long since become our culture, but our culture is beginning to abandon Christianity, proving that we humans will defend our culture more tenaciously than our religions." On the most optimistic reading, modern society would hang on to "its rights to Christianity as if retaining the rights to a piece of its own property". Overbeck saw "the basic cause of the present age's falling-out with Christianity" in Christianity's having lost sight of the once self-evident imperative not to be conformed to the world (Rom. 12:2). The expectation of the kingdom of God as an act of God, he suggested, was beyond the reach of modern humanity. At the same time, "Christianity..., like any other religion, is always dependent on the support of the culture in which it is rooted."[1]

The relevance of Overbeck's remarks to our situation today will be evident in the following examination of recent social trends and developments which have profoundly altered the way we live. How might the inculturation of the gospel be possible under these altered conditions?[2]

The "risk society"

A useful central theme linking together a wide variety of social trends and developments is the concept of the "risk society" developed by Ulrich Beck. He argues that the structures of the industrial class society are beginning to break up as a consequence of its own production. Just as modernization in the 19th century led to the break-up of a socially ossified agrarian society, so modernization today is breaking up the established forms of industrial society. Within the continuity of the modern age, society is being transformed.

The ecological consequences of Western civilization add up to a world of risks that know no bounds. The changes in modern industrial society have no less impact on its internal social structures:

> Modernization means surges of technological rationalization and changes in work and organization, but it also means much more besides: the change in societal characteristics and normal biographies, changes in lifestyle and forms of life, changes in the structures of power and influence, in the forms of political repression and participation, in perceptions of reality and norms of knowledge.[3]

Beck uses the term "individualization" to describe the de-traditionalization of our society, in which the individual is no longer guided by established institutions (marriage, family, state), but has become the sole architect of his or her own career. The consequence of this is a far-reaching transformation in social relationships. Instead of having to justify the break-up of a marriage, we have now reached the point where it is necessary to justify its survival. In place of the modern nuclear family, we now have the "negotiated provisional family". More and more children are growing up with only one parent or living alternately with one parent, then the other. These "patchwork families" have to make their way within a radical pluralism of opinions and values, from which they make their individual choices as and when required. According to Beck, this kind of individualism is not freely chosen, but is a logical consequence of our modern industrial society and its conditions of life — such as separation of the work and home environments, men and women both going out to work, the breakdown of social class hierarchies as a stable frame of reference, enforced mobility of the labour force, the influence of the media.

The modernization of industrial society is accompanied by an accentuation of social inequalities in terms of income levels and the distribution of paid employment. More and more people are experiencing unemployment for one or more periods during their lives. Those most likely to be affected are groups who are already disadvantaged: working mothers, persons with no vocational training, the sick, the elderly, foreigners and immigrants and semi-skilled young persons. But unemployment does not generate any new sense of class solidarity, being perceived as an individual hardship. The individualization of social risks has the effect of turning social problems into psychological states: personal dissatisfaction, guilt feelings, fears, conflicts and neuroses. Hence our society's current obsession with psycho-babble and psycho-remedies.[4]

Beck's analysis of the state of West Germany in 1986 has taken on added relevance and urgency since reunification. In particular, the collapse of the Communist planned economy in East Germany and the wholesale dissemination of Western structures without adequate provision for local input and guidance has placed severe stresses on the social fabric.

The "enjoyment society"

Building in part on Beck's analysis, Gerhard Schulze offers an interpretation of social change in terms of the transition from a society characterized by material deprivation to what he calls an "experience society". Though based on West Germany prior to reunification, many of his arguments could easily be adapted to the situation in other Western societies. According to Schulze, the fact that "the search for 'the good life' has become the central aspiration of people in our culture" is possible because of the shift from a society in which most people had to work mainly in order to secure the necessities of life to one in which basic needs seem by and large to be met and different sectors of the population seem mainly concerned with modernizing their experience within their specific milieu or sphere of life.[5]

Schulze argues that these milieus or spheres — such as the milieu of harmony, of integration, of self-realization or entertainment — are no longer linked together as they once were by universal bodies of knowledge to which the whole of society subscribes.[6] Even the label "Christian" can no longer be taken to indicate a commonality of personal experience extending across a broad range of the population.[7]

Only in the sphere of harmony, and to a very small extent in the milieus of self-realization and entertainment, does the

Christian element resurface — at the level, in other words, of the intermediate range of action. Instead of drawing on an established symbolic universe outside themselves to interpret their own situation, people become practitioners of do-it-yourself religion, relating self to situation in terms of symbols they pick and choose for themselves, often with specific reference to a particular sphere.[8] If we wish to speak of a common framework, it is the framework provided by a marketplace of various offers for personal enjoyment.

Taking Schulze's analysis of our situation a stage further, we might pose the question asked by Thomas Luckmann: is this marketplace of experiential enjoyment not after all linked to an overarching symbolic universe that furnishes it with a kind of religious canopy, albeit a slightly tattered one. Luckmann argues that the world of advertising conveyed by the visual media furnishes the dominant symbolic framework of our society, with its promises of a happy life and its suggestions of meaning. It is a kind of gallery lined with the contemporary icons of a secular religion lived out in the practical world. The central theme of this secular religion is the autonomy and independence of the individual.[9]

This theme of individual autonomy and independence is explored through various sub-themes tailored to the needs of specific milieus. One such theme is the promise of "home" and "domesticity", with the (unspoken) counter-theme of a widely felt desolation and loss of roots. Another is "life in all its fullness", "the young woman as an object of worship" — again with an unspoken thematic counterpoint: the avoidance of death. And finally, to take a third theme from this gallery of secular religious icons, one might refer to the promises constantly being made by the travel industry of "freedom" and "adventure". Again there is an unspoken counter-theme: the narrow circumstances and institutional restrictions which people cannot wait to escape from, at least for a few weeks each year.

In short, the marketplace of experiences and enjoyment is changing the secular religion that is lived out in the practical world. It is also changing the churches' scope for action, and the Christian "product" which they are offering the "consumer". Social change appears to be making the old religious maps entirely incommensurate with new perceptions of reality.

Pluralization

European societies are being shaped less and less by a single established cultural tradition. Western societies have become pluralistic, multicultural and multireligious, partly due to internal processes of transformation and differentiation, partly because of growing external influences.

In all the centuries since Germany was first Christianized there has never been a time when so many adherents of non-Christian religions have lived among us. A variety of political and economic situations has brought Muslims, Hindus, Sikhs and followers of other religions — workers, refugees and asylum-seekers, and others — to Germany in unprecedented numbers. Moreover, imported religions, particularly from Asia, now hold an enormous fascination for many Europeans, at least some of whom are willing to embrace these religions as an alternative to what they see as the stifling weight of the creeds and tenets and traditions of Western churches.

Despite these shifts, German culture, like that of Europe as a whole, remains very much under the influence of the Christian tradition:

> As potent architectural symbols, church buildings still shape the physical appearance and character of our towns and villages, the rituals marking the various phases of our lives are primarily Christian in origin, the Christian churches are an active presence in the broadcast media, while literature and the visual arts continue to take issue with the Christian tradition, often in surprising ways. Our calendar and our time-keeping are based on the Christian year and the Christian week. Marginal though its influence on the individual may be, the Christian tradition remains the defining context of our collective daily life.[10]

The extent to which Europe is still a "Christian culture", in spite of everything, can perhaps be appreciated only when one comes into direct contact with one of these other religious traditions in its own cultural context.

Yet the situation has changed profoundly.[11] In the wake of the process of individualization described above, the Christian tradition is itself undergoing a similar process of radical individualization and pluralization. The hallmark of this development is today's "patchwork" approach to religious faith, according to which people pick and choose from a range of elements taken from Christianity and other religions and cultures, looking for a form of religious expression that satisfies their own personal religious needs.

It is a matter for debate how far Germany has gone down the road towards a multireligious and multicultural society. But what is unquestionably new is the situation we now find in the religious marketplace, and the range of available choices and options for individualized religious expression, from the standard offerings of the churches to do-it-yourself forms of expression that people cobble together for themselves. While the Christian tradition remains very much present in German society, institutionalized Christianity as such, with its traditional doctrines, dogmas and denominations can no longer claim a monopoly on plausibility. Today Christianity appears as one product alongside many others in the marketplace. In the post-modern age, pluralism has become a radical philosophy.

But although the question of truth no longer seems to be an issue, the need for religion appears as strong as ever. The longing for guidance in a world of unmanageable complexity, the hunger for meaning and security in a hostile and alien world have not been diminished — quite the contrary, in fact.

Future prospects

While concepts like the "risk society", the "enjoyment society" and pluralization can help us to interpret contemporary social and cultural reality and the changes through which it is passing, they bring with them the risk of ignoring or neglecting other important aspects of that reality. Critics have pointed out that such buzz-words of the 1980s as "enjoyment", "experience", "life-style" and "risk" no longer reflect the mood of the 1990s. Heinz Bude insists that "anyone who still believes that the heightening of enjoyment, the refinement of life-style and the tolerance of risk are what life is all about has misread the signs of the times. People have become more realistic, less demanding — but also more insecure." In the face of growing economic and social tensions, "our feeling of ontological uncertainty has become more direct and existential", and "fate or destiny" has become "a defining category of the 1990s". And fate may include being a loser rather than a winner, to the extent of being rendered totally redundant and superfluous. [12]

The term "risk society" certainly applies to our political, economic and social situation, with consequences not only for people's behaviour and attitudes and the forms of social life, but also threatening the satisfaction of people's basic material needs and the survival of the natural environment. Unemployment and the dismantling of workable social security systems can lead to widespread impoverishment. Overexploitation of nature and the plundering of natural resources can upset the ecological balance and thus destroy the very basis of our life on this planet.

The analysis of our present situation in terms of the "enjoyment society", on the other hand, seems to start from the premise that we live in an age, not of want, but of superabundance. In fact, this superabundance exists only for a select few. Most countries of the southern hemisphere are excluded from it; many of them cannot even find the resources to ensure their own future survival. Meanwhile, in the risk societies of North America and northern Europe, the burden of social problems continues to grow:

> Material poverty does not normally feature very prominently in the writings of commentators on the present times. This is a

pity, because it is becoming increasingly clear that more and more sectors of the population are now being drawn into a downward spiral of social deprivation...

The so-called categorical imperative of the enjoyment society — "Experience your life to the full!" — is like a bad joke for at least 25 percent of the population in Germany, to whom such an injunction comes across as fatuous, insulting, cynical and inhuman. [13]

Rapid developments in the world economy, summed up in the term "globalization", pose a serious potential threat not only to the economy in Germany, but even more to the social situation. The surge of economic growth in countries like Korea, Indonesia, Mexico and Brazil is producing significant shifts in a range of industries, while the pace of international competition is becoming more intense. This is generating growing pressure to reduce production costs in Germany, which generally takes the form of reducing the provisions for social security. Deregulation, cuts in benefits that hit the most vulnerable members of society hardest, the redistribution of wealth from the bottom to the top and other developments of a similar kind, coupled with a high level of long-term unemployment, are creating a social situation in which the commitment of the social market economy to the common good is increasingly at risk. [14] There are no slums as such in Germany at present. But if unemployment continues at its current high levels, and more and more people are denied an opportunity to return to the labour market, while social exclusion and impoverishment are allowed to spread, then there are very real fears that whole areas of our cities will deteriorate into centres of misery. [15]

Taken together, all these things pose a major challenge for the churches. Given that foreigners and the poor are increasingly dependent on solidarity and support at the very moment when large sections of the population, driven by the forces of individualization, are losing any sense of solidarity and slipping into a "culture of narcissism"; and given that the churches can never separate themselves entirely from such social trends but are themselves a part of them; then the issue facing the churches is not just how they should relate, in a spirit of critical solidarity, to the "risk society", the "enjoyment society", religious pluralism or the victims of globalization. In essence, the issue is whether the Christian church is merely a reflection of all these different milieus and needs or whether it can fashion a role for itself in which ministering to spiritual needs and tackling social problems are perceived as the two sides of one coin.

It is also very much an open question how far the growing individualization and pluralization of religious orientation is a consequence of religious needs which are themselves a response to social and economic pressures and conflicts experienced by the individual. What is at issue here, certainly, is the extent to which the established or national church — the *Volkskirche* — remains an effective medium for religion.[16]

NOTES

[1] Franz Overbeck, *Christentum und Kultur: Gedanken und Anmerkungen zur modernen Theologie*, edited from his papers by Carl A. Bernoulli, Basel, 1919, pp.247, 273, 66, 7ff., 20ff., 10.

[2] Much of this chapter is based on Theodor Ahrens and Ingo Lembke, "Kultur und Evangelium", *Zeitschrift für Mission*, Vol. 21, 1995, originally prepared as a paper for the study group.

[3] U. Beck, *Risikogesellschaft: Auf dem Weg in eine andere Moderne*, Frankfurt/Main, 1986, p.25.

[4] *Ibid.*, pp.143-59.

[5] G. Schulze, *Die Erlebnisgesellschaft: Kultursoziologie der Gegenwart*, Frankfurt/Main, 1992, pp.34ff., cf. pp.425ff.

[6] *Ibid.*, pp.142ff.

[7] *Ibid.*, pp.364ff., 409ff.

[8] *Ibid.*, pp.346ff. See also Peter L. Berger, *Der Zwang zur Häresie: Religion in der pluralistischen Gesellschaft*, Frankfurt/Main, 1979, pp.39ff.; Ina Maria Greverus, *Neues Zeitalter oder verkehrte Welt: Anthropologie als Kritik*, Darmstadt, 1990, pp.222ff.

[9] Thomas Luckmann, *Die unsichtbare Religion*, Frankfurt/Main, 1991, pp.151ff.
[10] Karl-Fritz Daiber, *Predigt as religiöse Rede*, Munich, 1991, pp.58ff.
[11] See Rüdiger Sachau, "Die eine christliche Kultur und die vielen religiösen Lebenswelten: Widersprüchliche Tendenzen der Religion in der sogenannten Postmoderne", in H.-C. Bossmann, et al., eds, *Identität und Dialog: Christliche Identität im religiös-weltanschaulichen Pluralismus*, Hamburg, 1995, pp.144-59.
[12] Heinz Bude, "Schicksal", in H.Bude, ed., *Deutschland spricht: Schicksale der Neunziger*, Berlin, 1995, pp.7-12.
[13] Thomas Steininger, "Risikogesellschaft — Erlebnisgesellschaft: Aspekte zur Analyse unserer gegenwärtigen Gesellschaft", in *Religion — Macht — Kultur: Dokumentation der 2. Ökumenischen Sommeruniversität*, Rothenburg, Ernst Lange Institute for Ecumenical Studies, 1994, p.70.
[14] Although the focus of this pamphlet is on Germany, it should be acknowledged that the consequences of globalization are even more serious in many other countries. On the effect of globalization and the world economy, cf. Ulrich Menzel, *Das Ende der Dritten Welt und das Scheitern der grossen Theorien*, Suhrkamp, 1992; Dieter Senghaas, *Wohin driftet die Welt?*, Suhrkamp, 1994; Ulrich Duchrow, *Alternatives to Global Capitalism*, International Books with Kairos Europa, 1995.
[15] Cf. Georg Kronawitter, ed., *Rettet unsere Städte jetzt! Das Manifest der Oberbürgermeister*, Düsseldorf, 1994.
[16] On this see Volker Drehsen, *Wie religionsfähig ist die Volkskirche?*, Gütersloh, 1994; and Michael Welker, "Gottes Geist und die Verheissung sozialer Gerechtigkeit in multikultureller Vielfalt", in his *Kirche im Pluralismus*, pp.37-57.

4. New Testament Perspectives

Following this overview of historical developments in the German church and survey of the challenges it faces today, we now move to an examination of various ways of defining the church's role in society in terms of the relationship between the gospel and different cultural environments. The principal task is to identify those factors which the church needs to take into account in its efforts to inculturate the gospel today.

We propose to tackle this task in three distinct stages:

1. In this chapter we shall examine the biblical evidence to show that inculturation was already an ongoing process in New Testament times. From the light which the New Testament sheds on the relationship between the gospel and different cultures and on inculturation of the gospel in the true sense, we shall identify a number of basic criteria for the process of inculturation.
2. We shall then enquire (ch.5) how the results of our review of the New Testament are to be mediated in the actions of the church today. As a starting point for this discussion we have selected two contrasting models of the attempt by the church to define the relationship between the gospel and contemporary culture.
3. In the final chapter, we shall draw together the different threads of the preceding discussion and identify a number of elements that play a key role in the process of inculturation.

Since the subject under discussion is the inculturation of the gospel, it makes sense to begin by asking what exactly we understand by the term "gospel" itself.

In its original sense gospel means "good news". In biblical parlance it is the good news of God's actions towards humankind, bringing liberty and redemption, consolation and salvation, enabling men and women to live together in community and challenging them to give a new direction and purpose to their lives. For Jesus "the gospel of God" was the good news that the kingdom of God was at hand (Mark 1:15), that the apocalyptic rule of God was about to begin. In the preaching of the apostle Paul the gospel is the message of the cross and the resurrection of Jesus Christ (cf. 1 Cor. 1:18ff.; 15:1ff.). This gospel is preached — and experienced — as the power of God summoning human beings to belief in Christ and conveying the message of salvation to believers. For the New Testament the person of Jesus Christ, as the Son of God become flesh, is the very centre and substance of the gospel. The one gospel — the word is invariably used in the singular — derives its identity from this identification of salvation with the person of Jesus Christ.

However, it is already clear in the New Testament that the one gospel appears in a number of very different expressions or expressive guises. The term "gospel" has also come to be used as the name for a specific literary form, namely a narrative account witnessing to the coming of Jesus Christ as an event that brings salvation for all times. It is notable that the one gospel of Jesus Christ has come down to us in four different versions — the four gospels — in the canon of the New Testament, each one telling the story of Jesus with its own particular emphases. The gospel of St John in particular differs very clearly from the other three in its language and the world of ideas it inhabits. Instead of the kingdom of God, which is at the heart of the teaching and actions of Jesus in the three "synoptic" gospels, the central idea in John's gospel is the abundance of life that men and women will discover through the mediation of Christ. John is clearly writing for a different audience from that to which the first three gospels are addressed — an audience living in a different world of language and ideas and shaped by a different existential situation and a different experience of evil.

On closer examination it becomes clear that each of the three synoptic gospels itself represents a different approach to the inculturation of the one gospel of Jesus Christ. For all the similarities in the events they record, in the structure of the narrative and even in wording — and in all these respects they are much closer to each other than to the gospel of St John — there are nevertheless significant differences between the gospels of Matthew, Mark and Luke: differences in linguistic forms and narrative style and in the author's overall approach in terms of the audience he is addressing, the points he chooses to make and his theological interpretation. Each of the three presents the gospel of Christ — that is, the portrait of Christ and of the salvation that Christ brings — with different emphases.

The same remark can be extended to the other New Testament writings. They have been composed by individuals or groups who are attempting to convey the one gospel of Jesus Christ to people rooted in different linguistic, historical and cultural traditions who have to contend with their own particular existential problems. The gospel as proclaimed to Jewish Christians differs in tone and nuance from the preaching of the one gospel to the Greek-speaking population. The formulation of the gospel is determined in part by the cultural and existential context in which it is proclaimed.

This does not only apply to the incidental aspects of the gospel, but to its very core and essence, as evidenced by the history of the titles used to refer to Jesus — Son of Man, Son of David, the Messiah or the Christ, Son of God, Lord, etc. — or by the different interpretations of the crucifixion found in the New Testament. In the New Testament we encounter the one gospel in the plural, in the form of characteristically distinctive theological statements based on the writers' engagement with different contexts, temptations and challenges.

A number of important conclusions follow from this. In the first place, while the gospel is inculturated in many different forms both within the New Testament and throughout subsequent church history, the gospel as such retains a core identity. To adopt a deliberately broad definition, that identity consists in the fact that the preaching of the message of salvation is centred on the person of Jesus Christ. Given that different forms of inculturation are already apparent in the New Testament, we will need to proceed with caution in attempting to narrow down the definition of that identity.

Sometimes the relationship between the gospel and its forms of cultural expression has been likened to that between the kernel and shell of a nut. But it is simply not possible to separate the culturally formed shell of the gospel from its kernel. What we have here is more like an onion, with its successive layers. If we try to remove those layers, we shall end up with nothing. In other words, the gospel always confronts us in a specific cultural form. In the confrontation with a different culture, it has to be comprehended anew — and also formulated anew.

This reformulation or inculturation takes place within the specific context inhabited by the recipients of the gospel. That context is shaped by a variety of cultural factors such as language, symbolic universe, patterns of behaviour, institutions, as well as by the existential problems and challenges of the particular time and place. If people are to understand the gospel and take it up as "good news", it must be relevant within their context. If the gospel is not relevant to people within their specific context, in terms of helping them to organize and shape their lives, then the message is just so much empty verbiage, which will fail to get through to people and which they will thus reject.

So we have identified two criteria for the process of inculturation of the gospel, namely its relevance to a particular context, and the quest for the core identity of the gospel as such.

But where the cultural conditioning of the gospel is such that the core identity of the gospel can no longer be viewed as a straightforward known quantity, and the multiplicity of cultural contexts produces a variety of different expressive forms for the one gospel, then the question of how far the gospel is still recognizable as such becomes an urgent issue. Where are the limits of inculturation? At what point does inculturation distort or obscure the gospel message? This in turn is bound up with the issue of the basic unity of the church of Jesus Christ in different contexts and cultures. To what extent does the gospel, despite the impossibility of divorcing it from the specific context in which it is received, nevertheless succeed in forging a common bond between Christians in different contexts and cultures? And what can be done to avert the danger that Christianity, having been inculturated in so many different forms, will break up into a whole series of Christianities that end up drifting further and further apart?

Already the earliest Christian church found itself wrestling with these issues. This is often clearly reflected in Paul's letters, when he intervenes in disputes and urges his correspondents to abide in Christ. We see it particularly in the gathering of the apostles in Jerusalem (Acts 15; Gal. 2:1ff.) and in Paul's efforts to justify his mission to the Gentiles while at the same time reaffirming his fellowship with the Jewish-Christian church in Jerusalem. The New Testament is a primary source of evidence that the living and ongoing inculturation of the gospel is associated with a bold overstepping of boundaries which provokes critical responses from fellow-believers and excites controversy within the church. The fact that salvation is manifested in Jesus Christ for all people is not accepted without a struggle — not only with the opponents of the gospel, but also within the Christian community itself.

The success of inculturation evidently depends in part on its ability to irritate and inspire debate, and to provoke a conciliar argument about the truth. Ecumenical dialogue in the context of a shared understanding based on diversity and unity in the person of Jesus Christ himself is another criterion of successful inculturation. Essential elements of such a dialogue are the perception of fellow-Christians as a concrete expression of the presence of Christ, the shared need to wrestle with one's own entanglement in alienation and sin, and the recognition of mutual dependency in the quest for the identity and relevance of the gospel and the truth of the proclamation of Christ.[1]

NOTE

[1] See Ernst Lange, *Die ökumenische Utopie, oder Was bewegt die ökumenische Bewegung?*, Stuttgart, 1972, esp. pp.177ff.

5. The Church's Response: Two Models

As a starting point for looking at what action the church is taking to inculturate the gospel, based on the New Testament criteria outlined above, we might usefully recall the well-known typology proposed by H. Richard Niebuhr, writing shortly after the second world war. From his analysis of a series of archetypes for defining the relationship between Christ and different cultural forms, Niebuhr concludes that there are five basic models:

1. *Christ against culture*, a contrast, even a separation, between Christ and culture;
2. *Christ of culture*, a Christ totally assimilated into culture, a Christ who has become identified with culture;
3. *Christ above culture*, a Christ who comes before culture and takes precedence over it;
4. *Christ and culture in paradox*, a participation in culture coupled with a relativization of its importance;
5. *Christ as transformer of culture*, the conversion of culture to Christ. [1]

While Niebuhr's categories are undoubtedly helpful for understanding the historical processes by which the gospel and culture come into contact and sharpen our awareness of the variety of possible approaches to defining this relationship, they do, like most ideal typologies, run the risk of encouraging generalizations that blind us to the complexity of reality.

If we were to attempt a similar exercise today, and try to summarize in the form of models the conflicting views on the interaction between gospel and culture that characterize the present situation in Germany, we can distinguish broadly between two types. Again, each of these is an idealized model, designed to bring the issues into clearer focus. Neither of them — the "contrast" model or the "conformist" or "assimilative" model — exists in a pure form, and in practice each borrows certain features from the other.

The contrast model

The broad term "contrast model" may be used to summarize a range of quite different views on the gospel-culture relationship.

In German theological debate and in the church, Karl Barth's protest against "cultural Protestantism" has had an extraordinarily powerful influence. According to Barth, the merging of the gospel and culture was the original sin of 19th-century theology, leading as it did in the 20th century to the usurpation of the gospel by the National Socialists. Barth believed that the gospel is fundamentally not susceptible of inculturation, and that efforts to find a point of contact are misconceived. The essential "otherness" of the gospel is an immutable fact, resisting all attempts to "understand" or "assimilate" it. The gospel does not say what people want to hear: it confronts people with its own uncompromising message and demands and creates a hearing on its own terms.

While Barth thus dismissed out of hand the involvement of theology with culture and interpreted the gospel alone as the decisive guiding force for theological thinking and the pronouncements and actions of the church, other commentators have taken up this line of thought with different emphases and nuances. A few examples illustrate the nature of the concerns they raise.

The gospel and Western culture has been the subject of numerous publications by Lesslie Newbigin. In recent times his writings have become more widely known in Germany. [2] Briefly put, Newbigin's thesis is that at the time of the Enlightenment European cultures (as opposed to non-Western cultures) embarked on a road which is "not gospel-friendly". As W. Ustorf summarizes it,

> The thesis states that a fundamental shift in cultural assumptions has taken place in post-Enlightenment Europe. Modern culture has elevated human reason to a position of absolute supremacy, which has led to the adoption of a secularized, pluralistic approach at best, and at worst has plunged us into relativism or even nihilism. [3]

Newbigin undertakes a systematic critique of this Enlightenment climate of thought, which makes autonomous reason the measure of all things. By taking issue with a secular culture shaped by these Enlightenment assumptions, Newbigin seeks to give the Christian faith a new plausibility. Against the background of "pick-and-choose" philosophies and privatized religiosity, he calls for a renewed championship of the gospel as "public truth".

Whereas Newbigin's version of the contrast model sees the secular Enlightenment as the basis of modern Western culture and questions that basis accordingly, other writers focus their attention on the social structures that have grown up within European culture. Their critique is not directed at the autonomy of reason and knowledge as such, but at a self-interested knowledge that manifests itself in amassing power and wealth by suppressing and exploiting others. They attack the "culture of death", which destroys human life and marginalizes the values for which the gospel stands — values such as justice, peace and the integrity of creation.

In Roman Catholic theology, too, culture and the inculturation of the gospel have attracted renewed interest. Pope Paul VI's 1975 apostolic letter "On evangelization in Today's World" (*Evangelii nuntiandi*), describes the "gap between the gospel and culture" as "the foremost crisis of our age" (para. 20), and says that the evangelization of secular cultures is therefore the order of the day. To be sure, more recent calls for the "re-evangelization" of Europe have received a mixed reception even from Catholic missiologists, but there are many critical references to Western culture embedded in them.

The most vociferous criticism, however, comes from representatives of various forms of Christian fundamentalism, who see Western culture as dominated by pluralism and secularism.

Even this very brief survey makes it evident that the different positions from which Western culture is criticized reflect different theological convictions. And while they are all unequivocally critical of our cultural tradition, they tend to emphasize different aspects of the cultural tradition based on their own understanding of the gospel. But since all insist on the need for a change of direction and a change of heart driven by the spirit of the gospel, it ought not to be too difficult for proponents of different versions of the "contrast model" to enter into dialogue with each other.

While all who subscribe to this model are ultimately interested in the transformation or conversion of culture (to use Niebuhr's terms), we should be clear about the primary motivation behind each of these positions. Leaving aside the fundamentalist position, we may note that both Newbigin and the Catholic concept of the re-evangelization of Europe have been accused of regressive tendencies aimed at restoring the *status quo ante*. It is claimed that they are motivated by nostalgia for the *corpus Christianum*, for a closed Christian community, as well as by a desire — particularly on the part of the Catholic Church, but also on the part of institutional Protestantism — to maintain their social status, their influence over people and the power they wield in society.

To adopt such a position would be to ignore the individualistic-pluralistic realities of modern Western societies. But the concerns articulated by these various positions could also be taken on board in a positive way. Specifically, this would mean that the church is called to
— encourage Christians to stand up for the gospel in our world with courage and intelligence, thus taking up the views of Barth and Newbigin;
— stand up for justice, peace and the care of creation, and the socio-political implications of the gospel, thus taking up the concerns of Christians whose interest is focused on the conciliar process;
— stand up for values and standards without which a decent human society cannot exist.

In the future it seems unlikely that the unwieldy institutional structures of the established churches will be an appropriate vehicle for proclaiming such a view of the gospel. Instead we can expect to see localized communities of believers, Christian fellowships and pressure groups witnessing to the gospel in their area. As exponents of an alternative society — living out the "contrast model" in practice, as it were — such congregations will play an increasingly important role. But in emphasizing the contrast of the gospel to dominant streams of our cultural tradition they might run the risk of marginalizing themselves and being ghettoized as sects.

The conformist or assimilative model

In distinction to the "contrast model", others seek to recognize the signs of the times and take up social trends as an opportunity for the church. Surveys, studies in the sociology of religion and polls conducted among church members are used to keep in touch with people both inside and outside the church fellowship. Efforts are made to develop an appropriate framework and conditions to facilitate the communication of the gospel message. The underlying concern is that the witness of the church in word and deed might be failing to meet people's needs and that eventually the church might no longer have any basis for what it does. So what is at stake here is the modernity of the *Volkskirche*: its ability to compete in the public arena, its share in the religious market, its standing as the central agency of social welfare. And who would deny the need to develop the church's powers of persuasion?

Those who promote efforts such as these would certainly not bill them as emerging from an "assimilative" model. But the fact of the matter is that sooner or later every analysis of the church's situation, however sober and objective, comes up against interests of certain sections within the church and society. And membership profiles, which were initially designed simply to give a clearer picture of the way things are, imperceptibly acquire the status of guidelines for a "consumer-oriented" use of church resources. Recently, studies in the sociology of religion seem to have given way to marketing analyses. But in either case we are moving down the same road, with the results of opinion polls being used to determine the future direction of the church.

Unlike the "contrast model", whose starting point is the freedom and autonomy of God and the claim and the protest of Jesus — so that the contrast with the surrounding culture is often deliberately underlined and sometimes elevated to a point of absolute principle — the proponents of the alternative model do not generally have "conformity" or "assimilation" as their conscious aim. But even those who try to see the situation clearly for what it is in order to stand up for the gospel in the light of that understanding can easily find themselves acting under the dictates of dubious needs.

We are presented here with a number of different levels and patterns. Today many different currents of thought are coming together in the concept of the "open church", a church competing in the marketplace, which seeks to be present wherever people are struggling with their doubts and needs. In today's pluralistic situation it endeavours to present the Christian way of life as one way of life among others, and to proclaim the truth of the Christian faith with energy and conviction. But no longer does it claim to shape the spirit and character of German national culture. The church is a corporate player in the marketplace of religious possibilities, offering its wares alongside others. The process takes many different forms, and the "goods" on offer range from a choice of constantly updated religious experiences to a thoroughgoing critique of contemporary social policy or policies towards asylum-seekers.

If the pluralistic framework is pushed particularly hard in this type of approach, pluralism can cease to be viewed merely as a socio-cultural phenomenon within the church and a political requirement for the good of society as a whole and instead becomes a theological programme in its own right.

The emphasis is then placed on the church as the champion of vigilance against deviance, as the fosterer of a culture of well-mannered interplay between different market forces. Not wishing to appear sectarian, the church abandons mission in favour of pursuing the common development of basic religious truths in the marketplace of religious possibilities — truths that are claimed to underpin a whole variety of different religious systems.

The "conformist" or "assimilative" model seeks to engage with the changing socio-cultural situation. At the 1993 synod of the Evangelical Church in Germany, the US sociologist Peter Berger characterized this model in these terms: "Faith, theology and the church are reconstructed in a way that modern people, it is thought, will find plausible or relevant." It has to be said, though, that the manner in which this is done is often more pragmatic than theologically considered.

The price to be paid for conformity is high. According to Berger, this method "carries within it the seeds of its own destruction. The church finds itself making one concession after another. In the end, theology becomes indistinguishable from other fashionable ideologies of the day, while the church itself becomes indistinguishable from other socially acceptable and respectable institutions." In other words, the "core identity" criterion, the defining element that sets the gospel uniquely apart, is disregarded. The church simply does what others are already doing.

A certain irony attaches to a second critical point made by Berger. He argues that it is precisely the pluralism of the marketplace which ensures that the church "can never become a permanent marketing success or win permanent social acceptance. No sooner have theology and church been reconstructed in accordance with current philosophical fashion than that fashion itself becomes passé — the turnover of goods in the modern cultural supermarket being very rapid indeed."

It is very easy, of course, to criticize the conformist model. After all, who would willingly admit to being a conformist? The main concern of those who champion a modernization of the *Volkskirche* in this sense is that the church should face up to the fact that it always has been operating in a market situation, in all that it does. And since this is so, the important thing is to behave intelligently within that situation.

Some conclusions

A comparison, however schematic, of these two models makes it clear that each contains many unresolved doubts and difficulties. The "contrast model" seeks to preserve intact the core identity of the gospel, yet runs the risk of losing it. Emphasizing "relevance", the conformist model looks for points of contact between the gospel and society, and in doing so, it runs the risk of losing the specific character of the gospel among the generality of religious and every other kind of need. Both models have their positive features. Each emphasizes a key New Testament criterion for the inculturation of the gospel. But both also exhibit shortcomings that make them finally unsustainable.

There is something curiously abstract and static about this one-sided fixation on contrast and separation on the one hand, or on assimilation and identification on the other. Looking at the issue in terms of these models tends to imply that the gospel and culture are two finite and separate quantities which can simply be compared or contrasted.

One problem with this is the underlying assumption that we can ascribe a more or less homogeneous structure to the thing we call "culture". Perhaps this is still possible for some traditional cultures, but culture in post-industrial Europe is so nuanced and segmented that one can no longer speak of "European culture" as such.

But the main difficulty with this abstract juxtaposition of the gospel and culture is the failure to recognize that the gospel is always and everywhere an inculturated gospel, that it is never encountered in a "pure" form. The whole history of missionary activity shows that the evangelization or Christianization of non-European peoples has normally meant their "Westernization" as well. In other words, it was not just an encounter between gospel and native culture, but an encounter between two cultures. This is why it is important for theologians in the Third World to formulate their own theological concepts, in order to get the message of the gospel across to people in their particular situation.

The encounter with the gospel invariably takes place "in, with and under" (to borrow a phrase from Luther) specific linguistic forms, a specific narrative framework and specific historical, economic and social conditions. The Word of God is made manifest in human form. It is not vouchsafed to humankind directly. It is only made manifest within the context of a specific culture, where it comes to persons incognito and in an unexpected guise — just as Jesus did in his actions and words during his time on earth. In many ways the best way to define the relationship between gospel and culture would be in terms of the classic formula used to express the two natures of Christ: "not divided and not mixed". Gospel and culture can no more be separated than the divine and human natures of Christ. At the same time, gospel and culture must not be confused. As Barmen has taught us, the quality of revelation does not attach to the specific cultural or historical moment.

The shortcomings of these two alternative models suggest that the church would be well advised not to base its actions exclusively on either of them. The "core identity" criterion in the contrast model and the "relevance" criterion in the assimilative model need to be brought together in a relationship of creative tension which is constantly renewed as part of an ongoing dynamic process.

NOTES

[1] H. Richard Niebuhr, *Christ and Culture*, New York, Harper, 1951.
[2] See *EMW Information Document* no. 107, "Das Evangelium in unserer pluralistischen Gesellschaft", in which most of the papers were inspired by the theses of Newbigin, and one was written by him.
[3] W. Ustorf, "Die Beziehungen des Evangeliums zu den europäischen Kulturen", *Una Sancta*, Vol. 50, 1995, p.33.

6. Inculturation of the Gospel in Conciliar Perspective

Our critical examination of the contrast and conformist/assimilative models has clearly shown that the task of inculturating the gospel can only be understood as a dynamic process of linking together the gospel and culture, text and context, commission and situation. In this final chapter we shall identify and describe some of the recurring elements of this process of inculturation. Our attempt to summarize them in a systematic way owes much to the concept of "conciliarity".[1] We shall be taking up a number of important issues raised by the ecumenical debate, thereby contributing to a redefinition of the place and role of the church in modern society.

The following elements can be seen at work in the process of inculturation:

1. The courage to inculturate the gospel anew and the willingness to be subverted and transformed by the gospel and to allow it to open up new possibilities of life do not come out of nowhere. Both have to do with the movement that is grounded in God's revelation to Israel in the person of Jesus Christ. A recurring phenomenon in the Old Testament, especially in the writings of the prophets, is that the encounter with God that has taken place at a specific moment in past history is subsequently brought forward into the present, and heralded by the prophet almost as if it were a prefiguration of what is now to come. The revelation of God is not exhausted in a single episode or manifestation occurring at a specific time in a specific culture, but carries within it a latent significance that points beyond that time and place. Each new inculturation of the gospel emerges from or taps into a broad stream of narrated encounters with salvation and God and hopes to be made actual in the present time.

Recent ecumenical discussion has repeatedly stressed that inculturation is not simply a method or technique, but a trusting in the presence of God even in the midst of the transformations of our time, and a hope for the manifestation here and now of God's salvation as revealed to us in the person of Jesus Christ. The theme chosen for the 1996 world mission conference, which speaks of the one Christian hope to which we are all called, reminds us of this perspective and grounds the debate about the inculturation of the gospel in God's promise not to abandon the world to evil.

2. If the first concern is the recapturing of confidence in the gospel message itself, the second must be to emphasize the church's willingness to enter into and engage with the context in which people live. As Ernst Lange pointed out, it is precisely because of the commission to communicate the gospel that the church must concern itself with the actual reality of people's lives in terms of time and place, language and social structures. Since these factors have an important bearing on the successful communication of the gospel message, the church needs to engage with them. This cannot be done through an arbitrary attitude of "conformity" — as though real life itself were somehow an expression of the Word of God — but must emerge from a reading of the situation that is grounded in Christ. To emphasize the distinction, Lange speaks not of "conformity", but of an "adjustment into a specific commissioning situation". [2]

The church must therefore renew its efforts to understand the world around it, the cares and needs, the fury and the fears of people, in order to find out what witness it can bring to that situation, what it can specifically contribute, in contradiction or in confirmation.

3. The reference to an "adjustment into a specific commissioning situation", the empathizing with a situation, makes the point that contrast and conformity — or, more accurately, the imperative deriving from the missionary commission of the church and the situational imperative — cannot be separated. In biblical terms, the two belong together: thus shortly after the apostle writes, "Do not be conformed to this world", he adds, "Rejoice with those who rejoice, weep with those who weep" (Rom. 12:2, 15). If we obey the one injunction but disregard the other — and if we also ignore conciliarity as the third criterion enjoined upon us

by the New Testament — we run certain risks. Empathy may become conformity, conformity may lead to a loss of direction, a loss of direction may result in corruption of the message, and so on. This confusion of the gospel and culture plays down the gospel and fails to expose culture and society to its subversive and transformative power. At the same time, a critique of culture is possible only by engaging with it and actively taking issue with it.

4. What is needed therefore is a dialogical, indeed dialectical relationship between the gospel and culture. Confrontation, assertion and counter-assertion alone are not the way to go about it. What is required is rather a process of intensive discussion and debate with culture. We must engage with it, be willing to listen, hold up the claim of the gospel, learn from the resistance offered by different experiences and seek constantly to introduce the liberating perspective of Jesus Christ into the argument.

The attitude of the early Christian church to its cultural environment was marked by just such a debate. The revelation of God in Christ was used as an argument to reject demands for the circumcision of Gentiles: adherence to the Judaic way of life was not made mandatory, despite the insistence of conservative Judaeo-Christian groups. The moral beliefs of the contemporary culture were not rejected out of hand. "Test everything; hold fast to what is good" (1 Thess. 5:21) became the guiding principle in the encounter with the popular ethical tradition of the times. When candidates for baptism were told, in one baptismal formula, that Jews and Gentiles, slaves and those who had been freed, men and women form a new community in Christ (Gal. 3:28), this proclamation perpetuated certain hopes that were cherished by the ancient world — hopes for an end to ethnic-religious tensions, to the traditional allocation of roles between the sexes, to conflicts between social groups and classes. At the same time, however, these words outlined an alternative vision to the society that then in reality existed.

5. Inculturation is not simply a one-way street from the gospel to culture. Cultural changes may also prompt us to ask new questions to the gospel and to rediscover forgotten or buried aspects of the biblical message. Latin American liberation theology and the inculturation theologies of Asia and Africa all reflect popular movements to dismantle the structures of colonialism. The Western world, too, has witnessed social movements — such as the peace movement, the Green movement and the feminist movement — which have at times prompted controversial debate among church members. But this in turn has caused new questions to be asked of the biblical texts. Out of this has emerged an awareness that the received picture of the gospel was in part the product of human interests — political, economic, patriarchal — and to that extent one-sided.

Challenges arising out of cultural change should therefore lead Christians back to the Bible, and from the Bible back into the changed social and cultural situation. The hermeneutical circle of text and context, gospel and culture needs to be trodden each time anew.[3]

6. A critical interrogation of the churches' tradition regarding the quest for what the gospel really is today, a critical response to certain forms of church action and a critical questioning of the relationship that has grown up between church, state and society are of immense importance.

What was at one time a valid inculturation of the gospel can eventually come to seem outmoded and empty. No longer providing the answers to people's questions, which have changed in the meantime, it becomes a mere empty form of words, a "mummified version of the truth". The critique of "Christendom" and of our inherited understanding of the gospel — the criticism of religion (*Religionskritik*) — is an inherent part of the Protestant tradition, which forces us to reappraise the inherited pattern of Christianity. What becomes outdated in a new situation is not the gospel itself but a particular form of it, which now merely serves to ensure its survival without opening up any real new possibilities of life. The liberating power of the gospel itself, however, seeks to be made present and relevant within the new situation, that is, in relation to the problems and longings of people today.

7. The attempt to inculturate the gospel in a changing context in a new and authentic way is a dynamic and open-ended process. As such it always entails an element of risk. Inevitably, there will be differing views of the interaction between gospel and culture, culture and gospel. In other words, there will be conflicts. In the German situation, the need to engage with the social movements mentioned above has provoked disagreement. While some have seen the criticism of traditional "Christendom" prompted by these movements as the rediscovery of buried or neglected aspects of the biblical and theological tradition, and have thus welcomed the development of specific types of "contextual theologies" such as liberation theology, theology of creation, feminist theology, others respond with hostility to such moves. For those of a secular turn of mind, this engagement by Christianity with a radical critique of tradition and religion does not go far enough. On the other hand, those concerned about the survival of tradition and the unity of the church take the view that the Bible is being interpreted in a one-sided way and the faith and witness of the church called into question.

It is of the utmost importance to open our minds to this conciliar dispute and see it as a necessary stage in the quest for a fresh inculturation of the gospel. Only when the different groups ask each other critical questions and justify their own championing of the gospel to each other can understanding grow. And only by travelling this difficult conciliar road together will all groups be led increasingly to searching questions about the identity of the gospel and an understanding of who Jesus Christ is for us today.

8. The conciliar dispute about the truth — about the link between the gospel and culture on the one hand and the

critical tension between them on the other — is often difficult for the members of the churches, given their specific cultural backgrounds and perspectives. So it is all the more important to recognize that contrast and assimilation may evolve in different phases, the one succeeding the other in a particular rhythm or pattern.

There may be an initial phase of broad-based popular impact, when the gospel message picks up on existing trends and establishes a link with existing needs. Then comes a phase of moving the message into a specific communication framework and developing a structure of plausibility, in order that communication of the gospel can take place at all, and can be perceived as relevant. Next is the phase of critical review, when those involved ask themselves if the whole thing really is about communication of the gospel — or only about certain forms of human conformity. In point of fact, therefore, it is not a question of making a once-and-for-all decision to "join the right side" theologically, choosing between adopting current social and religious trends or critical-prophetic self-examination of the Christian legitimacy of one's position. It is more a matter of "keeping pace with God", as it were.

Let us try to illustrate this evolution of successive phases in an ongoing process with a contemporary example referred to in chapter 3. It may be that in their efforts to come to terms with the phenomenon described as the "enjoyment society", the churches in Germany presently find themselves at the beginning of this process: the phase of evolving understanding and incipient receptivity. Here and there churches are deliberately testing the water with claims to be "on the same side", interpreting individualization not only negatively as the dissolution of social forms, but also as a commitment to decide freely. People are experimenting with patchwork biographies for the Christian life too. But critical voices can also be heard, some of which we have cited above. In any case, it is evident that there is still some way to go before a distinctively Christian profile emerges within the "enjoyment society".

9. The final element required for the inculturation of the gospel in conciliar perspective is that the various social structures of the church should be co-ordinated and integrated — not only parishes, ecclesiastical institutions and ecumenical associations, but also the diverse strata of lay groupings, base communities and clerical leadership. Since the church is not a homogeneous body, inculturation is carried forward by a variety of different actors. We find pressure groups, discipleship groups, base communities, fellowship groups and the like coming together on the basis of a certain commitment and engagement and seeking to live out a special blend of "struggle and contemplation". The specific form of inculturation of the gospel to which they are committed cannot simply be taken over wholesale and adopted as *the* form for the church as a whole. The parishes, fellowships and institutional structures of the church are too diverse and varied for that. While the various groups challenge the church as a whole to be more decisive and clear in expressing the claims of the gospel, the church often provides them with opportunities for activity and leaves them sufficient scope for action within society at large.

The truth is that they both need each other. The official church is now in danger of asserting only claims that are so generalized that the "salt loses its taste". For their part, the groups are in danger of appearing overdemanding and prescriptive in their claims for others. What is needed is to develop a conciliar culture of dispute, in an atmosphere of mutual dependence and respect for the other's perception of the missionary task.[4]

Inculturation of the gospel in conciliar perspective underlines the character of the church as a dynamic and evolving community embarked on a process of discovery, learning and creative conflict under the banner of the gospel. The church sees itself as a movement seeking to discover God's mission in its particular time. As Dietrich Bonhoeffer said, "we must take the risk of saying things that can be questioned, provided they serve to stimulate debate about vital issues."